I0494028

The 5 Reasons You Have Struggled In Network Marketing

Discovering the things you can do to change your network marketing business for the better.

Success in MLM Volume 1

BY: Deacon Weeks

Table of Contents

1. You have not yet pre-qualified your leads
2. You do not understand the value of sorting rather than selling.
3. You do not have an attention getting campaign
4. You have not treated your business like a business
5. You do not actually believe that network marketing will work for you

INTRODUCTION

Your New Reality

So you have done it! You have gone against all practical reasoning, avoiding all of the "advice" from family, friends, and other broke people in your life... to start your network marketing company. It promises to fulfill your wildest dreams, and your deepest desires. You have this vision of firing your boss, zipping off on wild adventures in foreign countries, and doing all of your work from the latest technological gadget, on a remote beach. The dream of owning your own business is no longer a dream at all... you are the newest entrepreneur.

There are some things you do not yet understand, and you acknowledge this, but believe that the smart business decision was made... after all, your upline has assured you of this, and if anyone would know, it would be them. What will you do with your new found success? How will you spend all of the extra money you will surely be making? These are things that are still on your mind. Reality has not yet turned its often ugly head back toward you.

When I speak of reality, please understand, it is a matter of perception. You were brave enough to accept a new reality, but for how long will you be able to hold it? Will you actually "Fire Your Boss" before you see a single check? Most people, will not, and cannot. Instead, they will enter back into the comfort of the reality they have already made, and which they already have an understanding. As they try and wander back and forth between the reality they understand, and the one they are undertaking, they often find themselves all alone. This is where you are as soon as you start your own business. It is not what your upline has told you, they said that you would have support, and you probably do... it is just not the support you understand. As soon as you become a business owner, you have made a diametric shift in reality. It is no longer the responsibility of your boss, or management, or anyone else to keep you on task... It is yours, and it is now all about what you do. Yes, you make the rules, but you also get to take the blame.

You may be one of the few who can rise above the dangers associated with this shift in your reality, but you just as easily, and more likely are one of those who slip comfortably back into the reality of your previous life. You could cut off the communications from those who are trying to keep you focused on your business... but at the end of the day... it is your business, and not theirs. You will never be able to keep your wits about you and your focus on task, if it is the responsibility of others to convince you that the reality you are entering into is really worth your time and effort. You must decide right now, before another step is taken, if you are really... the newest entrepreneur, or if you were merely captivated by the reality of someone who is not you, and whom you could never become.

Are you still with me? Are you setting out on this brave new adventure? Then let us explore some of the things that will make us or break us.

Chapter One

You Have Not Yet Pre-Qualified Your Leads

The process of pre-qualifying your leads can be daunting for many people, yet it is absolutely essential for the network marketer. At the end of the day, it requires a certain sort of person to enjoy and succeed in the world of network marketing and MLM. If you simply assume that your reason for joining will be enough for anyone you talk with, you will be falling into a level of immaturity that could waste your time and the time of those you are trying to connect with.

Imagine you are a shoe salesman. You know all about shoes, and how important they are. So you find a spot at the edge of a desert, because people walking over hot sand will certainly appreciate your product. So you have set your shoe store up and you are pleased to see a customer stumble through your door. He is panting heavily, obviously right from the desert, and so a tinge of satisfaction overwhelms you as you set down your 32oz refreshment and attend to your patron.

"How nice to have you in our humble store, please try a pair of our comfortable sneakers."

The man shakes his head and stares blankly at you. He is obviously confused. "Sir, I am sure that you would benefit from our shoes… if only you would try them."

"No…. please…."

"But sir, I will satisfy your pains and your troubles…"

"Really?"

You see him break a smile and so you try another approach, "Yes, try a nice pair of sandals."

Now in anger he responds, "I do not want any shoes!" He leaps wildly for your 32oz refreshment and runs madly out of your store, drink in hand, never to be seen or heard from again.

So what went wrong? It is obvious, he was not in the market for, or ready to buy shoes, but you did not even try to find this out. Instead you assumed that he was right where you wanted him, satisfied in every other way, and ready for shoes. Had you understood who he was, what his desires were… you may have sold him shoes now, and for the rest of his life. If you would have known who he was, and how thirsty he was, perhaps you could have attended his primary need, and followed up with him once his thirst was well quenched. At least then, he would know you were kind enough to care about his suffering, and not simply trying to take his money.

In the extremity of this analogy we see the truth of many in marketing. They do not look at or consider the customer and who they are; they are too busy looking at themselves and their own needs to realize that by serving the needs of others, ours can be satisfied as well. Do not forget that your customer is not there simply to buy your product; they are real people, with real needs which may be very different from your own.

Network Marketing Is Not For Everyone.

All of the network marketing companies I have known will tell you never to pre judge saying, "This business is for everyone." This is a huge lie and not to be believed under any circumstance. Network marketing is no more for everyone, than skydiving is. Some people absolutely cannot skydive. Some simply will not even consider it, and others who do, have no business doing such a thing at all. Skydiving is not for everyone... neither is network marketing. Owning a business is not even for everyone, so how stupid are we to think that owning such a specific type of business is for everyone?

I agree, you should not pre-judge, but you better pre-qualify. Pre-judging is when I look at someone without any information, besides my impressions, and simply disqualify them. Pre-qualifying, is when I take my impressions and act upon them in order to discover if they are accurate. It works every way, in every circumstance. Let me assume that my customer wants to buy some shoes, which is a fair assumption. Now I must ask him, "What sort of shoes are you looking for?"

"I am not looking for shoes."

"Then what are you looking for?"

A wise man once said that questions are the answer. You must find the right questions, and the answers you receive will tell you whether or not your assumptions were true, and this will help you as you continue to build your business, and your marketing strategy.

Maybe he will tell you just what he is looking for, and maybe you will be in a position to help his primary need and bring him around to recognizing how shoes could benefit. Maybe not, if he simply does not want or believe he needs your product there is nothing you can do besides accepting the fact that even your wonderful product, is not for everyone. The worst thing you can do is try to convince him that it is. You must always find a way to make the prospect believe that they came up with idea they needed your product, mostly on their own.

It may be hard to accept, but network marketing is actually for a specific type of person. Your particular company is for an even more specific audience. To some this may be discouraging, to me it is very encouraging, and this means that a huge part of my job (and yours) is simply defining the perfect customer. Once that customer is defined, we can then go to work discovering where we might find them, in order to effectively promote our company. Up and to this point, you have probably not tried to narrow your focus because your well meaning upline has said, "Promote everywhere!" The point is, there are plenty of people to promote to, you do not need to promote in the wrong places, you need to find the right places.

The shoe salesman may be close to the right place, but he is miles away from the right prospects. If he were to do his research, he might find out that down the street there is a thriving shop which sells cold drinks, and food to those who wander in. As they are leaving, maybe they are looking for a place to buy a good pair of shoes or sandals. He could go there and offer a discount to people leaving the shop, or even set up a shop of his own across the road. With a little research he could find out where people who want and need shoes spend most of their time. In this way, he would not waste his effort on some poor sap dying of thirst that could care less about shoes.

You Have Not Been Talking To the Right People

When you realize how wasted your efforts have been, talking to all the wrong people, in all of the wrong places, you will run from everyone who has not passed your steps to become qualified. Finding out who the right people are is a task that comes from understanding your customer. You must become a hunter, defining the type of people who use your product based on all the available information you have.

It is like putting a puzzle together, you may know very little in the beginning. You have the box but it has not yet been opened. On the cover is a picture that you enjoy looking at, and inside are all the pieces that will give you a larger version of the image on the container. So you open the box and are immediately overwhelmed with all of the scattered pieces.

Some people in network marketing get to this point and say, "Wait, you told me this would be easy, now I have this box of junk that looks nothing like the picture. What do I do?" If you are at this point, do not get discouraged, the first thing you do, start separating and sorting the pieces. There are two types of pieces in the box, pieces with edges, and those without. Right now, you do not even have to look at the picture; just separate the pieces with the edges from those without. It is the same way in marketing. You take all of the information and look for the first step in putting your business together. It is usually right here in sorting the people you want in your business from the type of people you do not want, as the steps progress you can begin to get more specific, until you find the people and the correct places for them.

Consider this, you have all of the edges separated from the center pieces, if the puzzle is rectangle or square, there will be only four corner pieces. Find them and put them in place. These corner pieces are your foundation, they are like the first four people you need to begin building your company. They are essential in framing the structure of your company... you must try and place them in the proper location. If you do not get it right the first time, that is okay, in time as you build off from each one of them, it will be clear where they belong. You have to know who your four should be. You cannot (as much as you may want to) simply force a center piece into the corner... it does not work that way. It does not matter how badly you may want them to be a corner piece, they will not fit correctly, they will never be comfortable, and they will always fall back into the pile, waiting for the place they actually belong.

This analogy could be taken further, but the point should be clear, you must know who belongs in your business and where they fit. Some people try to take pieces from other puzzles and make them fit. This is completely ridiculous and all together impossible. If you do not learn anything else from me, learn this, network marketing is not for everyone. Your business is not right for everyone. The real business of your business is finding your customers.

A Pulse Does Not Qualify Someone for Your Business

There are a number of things you can consider when finding a way to qualify people for your company. This is based on a number of factors that you must determine. What is your product? Who is most likely to use or buy your product? Where do most of the people in your business live? What type of cars do they drive? Where do they vacation? The questions are endless, and finding an answer to each question you come up with, will take you a step closer toward your ideal customer. If we are going to hunt, we want to hunt for our ideal customer. Along the way it is likely that we will bag smaller game, but our goal should always be the prize, the trophy, the perfect customer.

Some people think that this process of qualifying is merely a game where we are trying to convince people how exclusive our opportunity is. There is truth in this idea, people are more attracted to something that is exclusive, and for a limited time, but it does not mean we have to take every warm body who comes through the door... we really should not do this. In time you will suffer for the choices made which were not made without forethought. The people who are wrong for your business at the outset, will most of the time be worse for it later on. They will neglect their duty, not understand what they are doing. They will spread all sorts of dangerous messages, polluting your team, and generally make your job harder than it needs to be. Not all customers are good customers.

I have family members in network marketing, which is how this industry found me, so it is possible that some family members are right for your business. The thing is there are a number of family members who have been involved in one or more companies with me, who had no business in the business. They always end up angry with you for involving them, and sour toward anything you have to say on the subject later. It is not that they found out some truth about how network marketing does not work. It is just that they were never right for the business, they proved this over and over again... and it never became right for them. It cannot become right for them; some people simply are not cut out for this industry. There really are people out there who need to be accountable to a boss, or even told how to do every part of their job. In network marketing, you are the boss, and that means you must keep yourself accountable and on task, no one else will.

This increases the importance of qualifying your leads. Not only will the wrong leads not be good for your business, they become toxic to it. These people can infect and destroy an entire team. Remember, they are working on the inside talking to many of the same people you would. When it all falls apart and it always will with the wrong people, they go to work campaigning against your business in order to validate their decision that it is no good. This is the reason for most of the bad press in network marketing, the wrong people in the business. Go to work putting the right people in your business.

Chapter 2

You Do Not Understand the Value of Sorting Rather Than Selling

It is not a hard to understand why people believe that they need to sell the business, there is a level of sales involved in network marketing. People are simply trying to sell the wrong product to the wrong people. First and foremost, understand what it is you are actually selling and to who. This points back toward the issue of qualifying, but sorting is another aspect of qualification. You must know how to sell your product once you get to the right people, but getting there is really where the hard work is done.

So, you have gone through the task of discovering who the right people are for your company, now you must get even more specific and more detailed asking yourself and them even more questions about why they would be a good fit for your particular team. Right now you are seeing the group that you must point your efforts toward. That information needs to be used to filter these people into your hands.

Throwing Paper at the Wall

This is the time and place in which you begin your fishing campaign. It is just like fishing really. First you have to discover the type of fish you are after. Next you find out where that fish swims around. Now you are looking for the right bait to attract that species in that place. The people who fail in network marketing do so because they forget this simple pattern. They are out there in the pond trying to catch some fish that does not live in the area... and then they get angry when they don't catch it. Or they are in the right place, around the right fish, but they are trying to catch them in their hands as they swim about sloshing and scaring the creatures. They don't have the right tools. Many are in the right place, with the right tools, but they are using the wrong bait, the right fish will not bite, at least not as often… but we are closing in on them, now it is time to bait correctly.

If you have the right business, and you are in the right place, all you need to do is bait your hook and wait for the inevitable. It can still be a slow and painful task, which is why most people start in network marketing part time. The trouble is, too often people get tired of waiting and they neglect the business. What happens if you are not there to catch the one that bites? It pulls away, slips the line or even breaks it; if you were real careless your pole is lost with the fish. Now you are even more frustrated and you toss in the towel. It is easy to get to this point, which is why everyone does not succeed in network marketing. It still does not mean that you will not, it just takes dedication.

We often talk of throwing paper at the wall in network marketing. When you have the right product in the right place, only then can you begin this part of your journey. It is about talking to people. You have to network in network marketing... or it is not network marketing at all. Many want the marketing without the network, does this really make sense? Talk to as many people as you can in the places where the right people are hanging out. I do not mean for you to simply say, "Hey join my company." No, I mean you really need to communicate with people, find out what they like, what they worry about, who they love, and what they dislike. This is very specific and comes only from the personal connections you make. As the relationship blossoms, you will see whether or not your business is still good for them. All along the way you will tell them things about your company and yourself because you are sharing your life as well. In time you will make the correct connections, and the people who are right for your company will start popping up all around you. You have basically risen up the ladder, changed your friendships and associations, and now your life will begin to change.

I do not mean that you will abandon your friends and family, but you will establish relationships with different people who serve a different need in your life. Think about this, you and Joe have always loved watching the Widgets play football. You go to games, throw parties with other widget fans; you talk about the team, its players, and their future. It is a relationship built around a common interest, The Widgets. If you try to make him into a person interested in your business it is likely you will frustrate the relationship that you already have. Now, it is not impossible to have friends who like your business and the team, but it is tough to change any relationship into something it naturally is not.

This is why it is best to find out what the relationship is about and what it is not about. You have to go through all of the previous steps and see if when you walk in the door of the right people, you find friends who you share other parts of your life with. You will both connect in this area too because you both appreciate that you are able to connect in another common way. If they are not there, it is probably not going to work out, no matter how bad you would like it to.

So move on, get in the habit of learning how to move on, how not to take rejection personally. When you are doing all of the right things in all of the right places, you will be throwing less paper at the wall, and so you will experience less rejection. You will still face plenty of rejection, but keep talking to people, keep building relationships. It is the only way to actually build your network.

Nailing Jelly to the Wall

Have you ever thought about how impossible this is? When you throw paper at the wall you are looking to see what sticks. If any does, you take the opportunity to build your network. However, you will run into difficult situations and people. Trying to fix them, change them, or make them accept your company is just like nailing jelly to the wall. It always slips over the nail, down the wall, and back to its original form.

There is no way to know when you do all the right things, who will join you and when. If you try to make them do what you want, you will almost always run into this problem. You have to let them come to you. Let's go back to our fishing trip. We had to hunt down everything, and it was work. We had to get the right tools for the job, we had to find the right place, and we had to find the correct bait. Even with all of this, some fish just will not bite.

There are good reasons (many of them) but who cares? You do not need to begin a campaign about why some fish will not bite. Is that your business? Could you imagine what would happen if you jumped in the water; hook and bait in hand screaming, "You will like it, just put it in your mouth!" That fish is not going to cooperate with you, it is more afraid now than ever... and for good reason.

When you have done it right, the fish walk up and put themselves on your line. They are saying to you, "We have a common union; I really do want to be your dinner." Now this is sort of a funny thought or image, but it holds up, the fish will fight once it is caught but in the grand scheme of the universe, he gave himself to you to be captured. This common union is one of the most beautiful things in the universe, respect it, appreciate it, and never apologize for it.

In this scenario, that is the end, you caught him, you wrangled him, cleaned him and you ate him. In network marketing, we catch them, wrangle them, clean them, and train them. The final step is the only real difference. If anyone teaches a fish how to catch other fish, I am on the first flight off this planet, to quote the Hitchhikers Guide, "So long, and thanks for all the fish."

Losing the Argument

Relative to the impossible task of nailing jelly to the wall is the point at which we begin arguing our point. It is as if we have shoved the bait in their mouth and seen them spit it out. Instead of wandering off to the next we try again and again. It is absurd, but it always occurs in this industry.

Think about a prospect who finds some criticism for the company you are promoting. Here you have done all sorts of work getting to the right place, at the right time, with the right people, tools, and bait; and your first hopeful prospect says something like "Eighty percent of the people in that company never make any money, you should do more research." You are so fed up that instead of saying "Cheerio Mate." You begin getting disgusted and forming arguments against this donkey's philosophy. "What do you know about it? This company is growing, as people make money the company grows and the scenario stays the same... of course the percentage does not change." There are thousands of ways to answer the argument, but few of them are any good... even if the logic is great.

Why is this? I do not have a clue, and I do not care. My job is not to argue myself into success, it is to find the right people, and if that person ever becomes the right person they will do so without your help. There is no argument or philosophy you can bring that will change anyone's mind for long. They must be able to take your philosophies and make them their own. If you want to be in the convincing business then be my guest, but I do not recommend this. It will frustrate you and them.

It has been often stated that when you argue you always lose. Think about this, if you win the argument you will always lose the contact... they did not want to lose the argument and will resent you. If you lose the argument you really lose because now you are abandoning your business and following a lemming over a cliff.

Remember that there is a huge difference in the person who is really asking questions verses them who are just trying to prove you are wrong. Inflection in someone's voice could be the only difference that separates the two. "Why is it that I have heard only twenty percent of the people in that business makes money?" Now you have a chance, "Great question, you see as the company grows and more people are successful, the percentage mostly stays the same. Let's say five people start a company and only one makes money. The other four add four each. Now all 5 are making money, the company has grown. There are 25 people in the company but only 5 are making money. The percentage has not changed. ($1/5=5/25=10/50=20\%$) The question is not about the percentage, it is about whether or not you can grow your company to be in the top percentage where the earners are found." That is the reality of network marketing growth and why those numbers exist, so I added it to help some of you visualize what your company really looks like. It does not change the point, if the questions are asked in the right attitude or spirit, they can be addressed. If they are asked in the attitude or spirit that is combative, or argumentative, you are better off not answering at all. Simply wish them luck and move along. I am serious here, really wish them luck, they will need it and instead of being angry or annoyed be the one who leaves the conversation on a positive note.

Chapter 3

You Do Not Have an Attention Getting Campaign

How is your offer better or even different than the thousands of others you see in this industry? One way to determine whether or not any value exists in your company is to step back and pay attention to what everyone else is saying about their company. If you hear all of the same rhetoric, it is quite possible that your company is not as rare and groundbreaking as your upline once told you. This is okay, it just means that you are going to have to search out and reveal the thing that separates your company, or better yet, your team.

Do not be confused here, the same language may be present in your MLM as many others, simply because that is the language of the industry, but it never hurts to altar that language for the sake of those who are not yet in the industry. The focus here is whether or not you can find a unique product, or a unique offer. Many companies already have this and you simply need to focus your attention on it.

Products are great for this; you can build a whole company on the claims of one great product. Good products make or break a company more often than people hope to admit. If a company comes out with some breakthrough nutritional product, you can sell a good portion of this product on the claims being made. The real wave comes when the product holds true to its claim and does what it claims or even more. MLM companies fizzle out and die often because they make huge claims about products that produce little in the way of results. Choosing not to be the guy, who sells potions that are not effective, will increase your credibility and your income. The purpose of MLM is residual income, if no one will buy the product again because it is lousy, than you have taken the long road to linear income. If you wanted to make linear income (Selling something one time and never making profit until you sell it again.) you should have kept your day job and not bothered with this MLM business.

The business itself can also have incentives that make it exciting to prospects, and differentiate itself from other similar companies. This is where a lot of companies actually excel. There are some pretty catchy and innovative attempts made to "Change the game," in network marketing. Many of these claims are real, compensation plans and bonus programs vary as much as personalities, there are similar traits but different organizations of these traits. One must truly be a wizard here, traversing all of the strange terms that companies find for describing the advancements. Be very careful to read the fine print, almost every company has some hidden bit of information that makes it harder to achieve success than they claim. The most common is product volume, it will almost always increase for you as you achieve levels of accomplishment, meaning you will have to buy more product or more services. This is not really some great evil devised by companies, it solves a larger problem. The only way to keep rewarding you for your hard work as your company grows is to increase what more successful members pay, because the money is being distributed among more people. You simply need to be aware of your company and how the system works. The reason they make this fine print, some people who would fail to sign up because of this, later learn that it is not a big problem, and continue the business happily. Any business that grows also has more overhead.

Be very careful though, because many companies with weak products and services rely only on the business itself. This is always a problem and you know it in your soul. The greatness of any company is never one single point; it is how these points work together. A company can have mediocre products and a great business plan, you're off and running, you have something to work with here. A company can have a great product and mediocre business, you have great potential here. If a company has a great business and a terrible product, you have the biggest chances in the world of being very disappointed as your company fails. The product is the true foundation, even though it may not be what you are selling, it is the foundation, and it must be strong enough to hold your building. The analogy works; you might build a huge group based on the business, until people ask about the business itself, which it is always the product. The product needs to be purchased over and over again, in order for the business to work. When people near the foundation that are not making much money, if any, stop buying the product because it sucks, your whole organization begins to crumble and it will not be long for this world. Best case scenario is you keep putting in new people at your revolving door. Do you think you can keep this up? You have just gone back into a linear income business.

It is actually much better for your business to have a great product and lousy business plan, you can still sell the product for a decent profit in most cases, it is sort of linear, unless people really like the product. They will keep coming to you and you can realize some decent profit, even build your own little niche of customers. You do not have this option with a company who has terrible products; they will always fail you in the long run.

Everyone Has the Best of Everything

You may believe that your product is the best there ever was. It may even be the best there ever was, but how do you transfer this idea from yourself over to your customer? It does not really matter what you think, it matters what they think. Your customers will always sell your product much better than you can. They will also destroy you and your company very quickly if you are not careful. Remember that people can be very emotional about the things they purchase; you will never bring your product up by knocking down another product. You can still use other products to sell yours.

Tabitha sells cookies. She is convinced that her cookies are the best you can find. Her competition is actually The Girl Scouts, they have some great cookies, but hers are made fresh and even tastier. She could say, "Girl Scout cookies are dry and bland compared to my cookies." Some people will try hers, but they already have a bad taste in their mouth, Girl Scout cookies are pretty darn good, and when you buy them you feel like you did something good because you helped support little Susie down the street who just wants to go to band camp for her summer. This is tough marketing to beat.

A good tactic for Tabitha is to ask the question, "Do you like Girl Scout cookies?" If they say yes, "Great, try these, they are our own recipe of some of your favorites." If they say no, "Great, try these, we feel they are an improvement of similar recipes." Either way she gathered just enough info about the customer to properly serve them, without bashing the other product. Being an improvement on an old favorite is never bashing, just be careful that you use this with the right customers. If she would have said this to the other customer, it could have had a bad outcome. People do not want to believe that the products they choose to use could be improved, that implies they are not smart enough to make a good decision on their own. Never make the customer feel this way. Your recipe may be better, let them tell you this. Yours may be simply added to the purchases they already make, which is okay also.

Relate this to your MLM Company; never go out bashing other MLM companies, or their products. The best you can do is turn some of the marketing that exists toward your company. "We have a product similar to....." part of your research is to find out what they use already, and then get them to try your product. Some MLM companies use services and not products, usually it is as simple as saving them money on a service they have already decided they enjoy. This can still be tricky since people have to go outside their comfort zones in order to switch. Do not let this bother you too much, it means that when they do switch, it will be even harder for anyone to turn them away again. People get comfortable with the products and services they use, it is like a habit to pay that bill or buy that product every month. In time they even forget where they heard about this product. Even if they become team builders, they do not think much about how their upline sold them on a product or service, they think mostly about how they are using their own products to benefit their own business.

You Have Not Targeted Your Campaign

Back to this we will always come. Just as you had to learn to find and qualify your leads. You must learn to target your campaigns. It does not make sense for Tabitha to be trying to sell her cookies outside of the same desert that brought a hapless traveler into the shoe store earlier. The customer may be hungry, but cookies are generally a dry product that increases our thirst… and we know he is thirsty enough already. Target your campaign to the right audience. If you put up a bill board for your cookies outside that desert, you are still asking for trouble. The potential customer will always associate your product with his misery.

Bring it back down to reality, where does your customer go, what do they do, how do you get your campaign in front of them? These are all questions that need to be asked again and again if you hope to advance your network marketing business beyond the realm of a hobby you tell people about, verses a business that makes you real money. So before you go about running a campaign, think about who your campaign is targeting and how they are being approached. A campaign about great cookies must be targeted toward people who eat cookies, or have eaten cookies already. If you plan on marketing to people who do not generally eat cookies, than the campaign should not actually focus on the cookies at all.

Tabitha just discovered something profound. She has learned that she can market to people who love to try new things. So she created a campaign that talks all about the newest thing, something that very few have seen yet because it is so new. She starts out not even revealing that she sells cookies, it is all about the process and the new formula. This campaign is not directed to cookie lovers, they would be frustrated by this; it is pointed right at the people who always want something new.

By creating the right type of campaign for the right audience you will always convert more of your leads. This is a bit of a magic formula, but like all magic formulas I have seen, it takes a whole lot of work to make the magic pour out. It was never the direct sales work that destroyed most in this industry; it was the back breaking work that leads to it. If anyone told you this before you were involved, you may have run from them and never become involved in network marketing. You see, they targeted you with the right campaign, to get you in the door. The thing is, they were not really wrong about you, it is just that you are not giving yourself the chances you deserve to make it work for you. Believe me, I know that it is really hard work, as hard as any job, but in this job, if you do it right... you will get paid when you stop working. People do it, you are a person, and you can do it too... but no one will give it to you.

Choose Your Words Wisely

This is always good advice, especially when we consider your network marketing campaign. You must always know how to speak to your customer. It is not always in an easy going manner, you are the investigator, and you need to know how your customer might react. The only way to learn this is to get in there and start talking to people. It is important that your words are alive enough so that your customers do not go to sleep on you. Remember, most people do not retain much of what is being said, they will remember a few key points and that is about it.

When I begun to learn about art and drawing, I found out why it is that so many people struggle to draw what they see. The trick is that they do not really know what they are seeing. They believe what they are seeing, but they really have no idea how it actually looks. Some people can actually see the truth of the world around them, and then they can duplicate this in a drawing when asked to, but they are the great artists who either do something great with what they have or simply let it slip away into oblivion. The truth is, we can all be taught to see correctly, even to the point that it would improve our artistry, and that is what I am after, helping you to take off the goggles, so that you might see correctly.

Did you know that there are no lines in nature? Yet, if asked to draw anything it begins with a line. Technically, there are lines everywhere, even in nature... but they are not lines like we see on paper, they are edges that roll into something else. Begin to see this in your world, from the smallest to the largest objects. Even the ink on the page is merely a lifted edge which rolls into something else throwing a shadow here and there. When you look out onto the world, you see shapes and lines and that is all your brain can seem to process when you try and reveal what you saw. No one has a round head, but every child will try to perfect his circle when he first sets down to draw someone. The eyes are just as round, but they are never round at all. Are they oval? If you think so, then you still cannot see your neighbor. The shapes of nature are imperfect and oblong. Nature is not really about shapes at all, but the endless flow of shadow and light. It is about what you see, and seeing it as it really is. When you do see it correctly, you can become a creator yourself. You can sit down and lay out a creation of your own that will tell the person who looks upon it, "This makes sense."

Nature always makes sense, even if we hardly ever notice what we actually see. The masters of art, they have captured the truth in the form of a lie. The painting is never real, but it looks that way and so it makes sense. In marketing, you are always doing something similar; you are speaking in the language that people can understand so that you might get their attention long enough to have them understand you and your product. You are learning to use the common information inlet, for the purpose of a lasting connection.

The act of falling in love, it has long been the subject of everyone who listens to their muse. When you fall in love with someone, it is because you have allowed yourself to look past the common shapes and forms, and to actually see them for who they are. Consequently, the ability to truly love anyone is reduced down to being able to know the truth of them, and accept that truth. It can be really hard to find that truth, and even harder to accept what you have seen, but that is the secret of love... and marketing. You must be as real as you claim to be, in order for anyone to stay with you for the long haul. Many have wooed their partners, few have kept their vows.

Choose your words wisely, and always keep your vows to your client. It is your job in marketing to woo your customer. It is your job in business to keep your vow. If you combine these two principles, you will increase your success rate in any business you put your hand toward advancing.

Chapter 4

You Have Not Treated Your Business like a Business

Most people play at network marketing, it is something they do here and there, and something they plan to get serious about someday. Then when three years go by with no profits, but actually losses, they turn on the company in a rage, "You promised this or that!" To which the company replies, "We promised nothing, read the forms you signed." No company has gained friendships by saying this to the angry customer, but it had to be done. That person never took the business serious, you know how I know? They blamed the company for their failure. The minute you set out on a network marketing company, you were told you would own your own business. That may sound very exciting to say, but it is a fancy way of saying, "Own up to it buddy... you have no one to blame but yourself." That is what owning your own business, is really all about. The guy who gets angry with the company is the one who never owned his business at all. He was relying on fate and circumstance, but they failed him, so who does he blame? Not himself, but the company, the same one who warned him when he was caught in the frenzy, "We are not making income claims." At that time the information was disregarded, "They are not talking about me... that is the other guy who struggles to succeed." For a moment you believed it, and you were wooed... but did you ever take your vow serious?

If you did, you would not have tried to become a customer again, by blaming the company when you did not succeed as you had hoped. If you take the vow serious, you should take your business serious. That means that you must actually treat it like you would a real business. Welcome to being self employed, you will work long hours for little to no money...

often losing money as you go… all in pursuit of that day in which you become profitable. It is always out there, but the window is always closing. Will I become profitable before I go completely broke? The race is on now my friend, and doing nothing will certainly take you to the poor house.

Establish Your Intentions and Goals

What are your intentions and goals then? If you are going to get serious about your business, then you need to become serious about what your intentions actually are? This is not all about what your dreams for your life and business consist of; it is mostly about what you see your business doing consistently with a little bit of work. For every intention you have for your business, you must have an action associated with moving in that direction. If there are no actions that relate to your intention then they are not real goals at all just ideas that could someday come to be.

Of course, you must understand that the idea always precedes the action, so go ahead and define the idea. In this stage, or soon after, you need to determine what actions are required to reach the goal. When you take the intentional step to relate the goal with a specific action, the actual execution comes very naturally. When you create the idea without the action associated with it, you are actually confusing yourself and all of your motion becomes quite futile. It is possible that in your pursuits, you run right into the proper actions, but it is the long hard road. The road is long and hard enough; do yourself a favor by connecting your intentions to your goals, and your goals to your actions. This circle will reconnect and keep you moving in a positive direction.

You have an intention; you create a goal, attach an action, and then relate your action to your intention. If your action meets up to your intention or defines it in some way, then you know that you are close to achieving your goal.

Let's try this; I intend to make money. My goal is to add $200 a month to my income. My action is to sell soap. As a subtext the act of selling soap requires its own formula, of which we have earlier discussed, finding the right people, etc. When I sell the product I will begin to make money... which was my intention, and which has brought me closer to my goal of $200 a month. This is how the cycle works... it is as simple as that.

If I intended to make money and then went off selling soap, I would probably make money but without goals, the work would become frustrating. Humans need a goal to focus on, and when they reach some, they must always make more goals. When they fail to make more goals, they become annoyed, frustrated, and end up making a mess of their lives. Most of the cases of addiction in our society are a direct result of people having no real goals for their life.

If I have a goal and an action without any direct intention, then I become really frustrated as the realization of my goals are not met. What happens is quite interesting and should be further studied, but the individual will be getting closer to their goal every day, only to ruin themselves just before they reach the goal because it does not feel like they are accomplishing anything. Others can say that they are accomplishing something, but they cannot see this because they are fixed only on the goal itself. The intention is a bit less specific, and it is the bridge that keeps one moving toward the goal itself. In the first month I may only make $50, if you have only the goal in mind you are angry and may throw in the towel because you did not reach your goal. If you made $50 and realize your intention was to make money, you are happy enough to keep moving toward your goal.

Finally, if you have the intention to make money, and the goal to make $200 a month, but you add no action... you will get nothing. This is the fate of most that jump in to a network marketing business. They have intentions and goals, but they have no action. How did this person ever believe they would be successful, they may have wanted it abstractly, but they never believed it. If you believe something, you will act upon that something.

Organize and Structure Your Business

You must now think of your company as a microcosm. People do not think much about organizing their network marketing business; Most of the time it seems as if the company has done a good enough job at this for them. The company has supplied you with outlines and training materials, but if you do not utilize them, they are of no value.

You must learn to recognize the different areas of focus in your business. There are many ways to view your business, it is yours and for you to decide, as a starting point think of a few basic divisions. Lead generation is an important area of focus, next you will have to market to the leads, followed by closing. Some will stop here, and I do not recommend this. Once you have customers and partners, you need to design training divisions, and organizational departments which recognize and utilize the strengths of each team member. You are a team builder, and when you run into people who are interested in your business that are not team builders, you had better find a good spot for them, or they will become one of the many lost souls in the network marketing industry.

At first, it is probably just you, and you must fill all the roles. At this time you are learning about your strengths and weakness. You should always recognize your strengths and use them, while sharpening your rougher edges.

The thing to remember about your weaknesses is that others in your organization will have these as their strengths. Building a team is always about placing the people where their strengths can be utilized. When you do find the other team builders, you can share your working model and get them on the track to building their own team. They may want to build their team in a totally different manner, this is okay, and there are a number of ways to get the job done. Simply be available for your team builders if they are struggling and need your help. Almost every business comes down to its organization, how can you build if you have no idea where to put the pieces? Your business is not a pool party where everyone is swimming aimlessly with different ideas in mind. It may seem this way, but it cannot grow this way. The people in your business must be unified under some common structure and goal. If they have only their own goals in mind and cannot see that the way to their goals is through the companies, they are probably wrong for your business. Trying to make people right for your business will always frustrate you. The only way you make them right for your business, is when they are willing to be taught... in which case they were more right than wrong.

Dedicate yourself to giving life to your creation

Your business goals must be defined in your mind, and this vision must be put forth into the world where concept becomes reality. No one is going to build your business the way you want it for you. At best, someone builds a business you are a part of, and you have gone the long road to becoming an employee. Granted, I believe that many in network marketing ought to be in the position of employee because they cannot handle being the boss. Maybe this is you, and great if it is, but you better at least find someone in your organization who can lead. If you cannot... it is either going to become you, or your business will fail.

I believe that becoming the leader is what turns a business around. Some think this is about turning away everyone else and doing it all yourself. You cannot do it yourself, certainly not in network marketing. If you try, you will add a few people, and they will just fall away. If you recognize your need for leadership you can build the business you dream of now. Leadership is all about taking the people with you on your adventure. Some will not go with you, but others will see your vision and hope to be a part of this.

I love the Bible; I have read it cover to cover more times than any other single book. There are great nuggets of wisdom to be found whether you are a believer in this or in that. One is in Proverbs 29:18 "Where there is no vision, the people perish..." You must have a real vision or your business will perish. Yet it does not end there. "...but he that keepeth the law, happy is he." Now Biblical scholars will scorn me, but I believe it is our right to apply scripture to our life and circumstance. The law, in our situation, is the building and organization of our business. The law is any foundation you create. Your foundation here is the structure of your company and it becomes the law... keep your law and you will be happy. If it becomes time to build a new law, it is only because your old law was not sound. Make it sound, build it, keep it... and you will find success.

This is not just some passing fancy; you must actually dedicate your life to seeing your vision into a reality. You must organize yourself in every way which leads you to your vision. You must remove every way that leads you away from your vision. The first part is finding out which way leads you toward, and what things pull you away. No goal can be realized until you take the time to clear the way.

Too often people will have an idea and just let it die there. They refuse to give life to their creation. It is always a thought or an idea and never an actual entity. Your business is a living entity that will live or die based on how well you care for it. You birthed the idea; if it is still a good idea, let it grow, do not simply kill it out of some fear or another. Take the time to set up your business properly; realizing all of the ways toward success and staying true to the course you have set. If you have to deviate, so be it, survival is sometimes that way. You must always be course correcting as you are on your way. The first step here is to figure out what things lead you to your goals. The second step is to apply the necessary movements. The third step is to adjust as needed. It really can be that simple.

Chapter 5

You Do Not Actually Believe That Network Marketing Will Work For You

This becomes the heart of most failing network marketing businesses. You wanted it to work, you tried to make it work, but you did not believe that it would. If you cannot get over this hurdle, your network marketing business has little chance of doing much more than annoying you and everyone around you. Most of the training for network marketers actually begins here. You have probably heard more about this than anything else. The problem is... if you have no understanding of some of the things that make a good company function, you can hardly shift your thinking into a place where you might actually believe that the business will work for you. Now that you have some of the fundamentals concerning your business, it is time that you learn to actually believe that it can and will work for you if you apply some key principles.

Million Dollar Fantasies

Before we get too far into encouraging you with a lot of Ra Ra Ra, we are going to address some of the things that keep people from being able to believe the message in this industry. Most of the talk about belief comes down to playing on your imagination. Can the average person really comprehend owning private jets, and 40 foot yachts? It is not my goal to burst your bubble if this is a dream of yours; it is my goal to reveal in you whether you are even capable of shifting this dream into a reality. Big dreams are great, but can you make the shift from big dream to reality?

The key here is to write your big dreams out. They can be as wild as you would like. The purpose of this is to recognize the truth or falsehood in the reflection of your words. Once you are able to view the dream outside of your mind you can begin to put some wheels to it. It is important that you begin to look at your list in a more managerial way. Determine what your most important dream is. Then determine which dream is your easiest to obtain. Once you have begun to find the dreams that you can obtain, the ones that feel real to you, focus as much attention on these dreams as you can. Begin to plot the steps that will bring you to the achievement of the dreams you can really wrap your mind around.

When you start to focus on some of the smaller or more obtainable dreams, as you realize them, you will be able to cope more with accepting some of your larger dreams. Too often people hold their focus on some huge dream, and the longer it goes before they are closer, the more frustrated they become. Do yourself a favor, focus on the dream that you can realize. When you realize the first dream, the second dream will reveal itself. This principle will repeat itself until one day you wake up and realize that you have obtained many of your dreams. You will always have more dreams… that is never the problem, you simply need to recognize when you are accomplishing one.

All That You Allow Yourself to Have

Like it or not all that you are and all that you have is a direct result of your responses to your circumstances. Everyone has different circumstances, and different struggles, but where we find ourselves is not simply a result of our circumstances, but our responses to them. This cannot be overstated, and so it will probably be repeated as I go forward.

I have heard people compare the "advantaged" with the "disadvantaged" a number of times. I can even remember a teacher in high school once telling us with all clarity, "There is no such thing as equality, one man is born a king and another is tossed away, growing up in foster care and poverty. One boy is born healthy and another has no use of his legs, or is blind. Can anyone say with any confidence that a person with a disability will have as easy a time obtaining the American dream as the healthy?" Many times I have thought about what he said, because he was not telling us that we should simply lower the bar for these people, he was trying to show us how they have often risen above the limits set by average men, in spite of their "limitations" yet I know healthy men who will speak only of their limits and not understand that the bar has been self imposed.

Everything that has been achieved in life is the result of someone reaching above and beyond a limitation. Greatness is achieved by those who look at the bar and say, "I will rise above." You may not have what you consider to be some great task before you, or perhaps you do, it does not matter... you are a human being endowed with creativity and strengths whose limits cannot and have not been measured.

Every time someone sets a limit on the abilities of men, someone comes along and graciously breaks through. I can say today that man will never run a mile in one minute, or one second, but I hold my tongue at the knowledge of the 4 minute mile. When one man broke through, many followed. We have reason to balance our creativity, and there are extremes they may never be met... but man will not stop inching closer and closer toward the loftiest of goals.

Can you hear the chains breaking around your own soul and spirit? You will be met with adversity and struggle all along the path toward your desires and goals, but you are in great company, all great men and women have faced adversity. The greatest among us will never focus on that adversity, but they are always thankful and humble, accepting without apology the rewards that a life well lived offers up. I say well lived, and I mean this, for most men never live at all, they simply function and exist, never trying to upset the status quo. You have not made it this far because you want only to survive; you have made it this far because you hope to thrive.

Overcoming the Hurdle

Every man woman and child who comes into this world is given a hurdle to overcome. I cannot say that there is only one, I cannot tell you what yours might be. I will not tell you about mine today, I will only remind you that the human experience is fulfilled by working to overcome. What we have to overcome is as various as we are on this earth. The genius that we see around us every day, even the things we take for granted now, are a result of humans overcoming the hurdles.

Consider the life of a human being. He is born helpless, and requires the attention of other humans simply to survive. In the beginning he overcomes the hurdle of helplessness. Some think they have always done it themselves, and so they never seek the help of others. Be humbled in this, even the unloved who survive long enough to say they were unloved, were cared for in their helpless state.

As the child grows they learn to be independent. They face things like weak muscles that cannot hold their weight. It is painful and difficult to stand, yet the desire to be free and mobile is greater than the pain of growing muscle strength. This is always the way it goes; the desire for one thing must outweigh the pain of another. When it does, you are on your way to overcoming... when it does not, you will not move from the strength you have achieved. Many reach for comfort over achievement, and at some time... in some place we all will... but today is not the day for me. The question you must answer for yourself is whether or not you have achieved all you hope to in life.

I have told you that the Bible motivates me, and there is one section that truly inspires. In the book of Revelation there are two chapters which deal with seven churches, their struggles and their rewards. They are chapters two and three, and each address to each church ends with the same statement, "To them that overcome…" The address echoes through the ages and through my own soul, "To them that overcome…" The rewards of life are always on the other side of struggle, and to them that overcome are given the gifts of success. All the tools to overcome have been provided but the act of overcoming and applying is always up to you.

So I leave you with the same address. To them that overcome are given the fulfillment of their life's desires. This is an inward statement that must have the legs of outward actions. Just as the athlete must train and believe, so must you. Remember to pre-qualify your leads. Always understand that you are sorting rather than selling. Create an attention getting campaign. Treat your business like a business. Finally, you must believe that network marketing will work for you.

CONTACT ME:
happyfortunehunting@gmail.com

www.secondwavedownlineclub.webs.com

www.ingramcontent.com/pod-product-compliance
Lightning Source LLC
Chambersburg PA
CBHW051817170526
45167CB00005B/2055